Contents

Classic  Cookies

Gooey Thumbprints

1 cup (2 sticks) butter, softened
½ cup powdered sugar
2 tablespoons packed light brown sugar
¼ teaspoon salt
1 egg
2 cups all-purpose flour
¼ cup jam

1. Beat butter, powdered sugar, brown sugar and salt in large bowl with electric mixer at medium speed 2 minutes or until light and fluffy. Add egg; beat until well blended. Add flour, ½ cup at a time, beating well after each addition. Shape dough into disc; wrap in plastic wrap. Refrigerate 1 hour or until firm.

2. Preheat oven to 300°F. Shape dough into 1-inch balls; place 1 inch apart on ungreased cookie sheets. Make small depression in each ball with thumb; fill with heaping ¼ teaspoon jam.

3. Bake 25 to 27 minutes or until tops of cookies are light golden brown. Cool on cookie sheets 1 minute. Remove to wire racks; cool completely.   *Makes about 3 dozen cookie*

Variation: You can also use chocolate hazelnut spread or chocolate spread to fill the cookies instead of jam. Prepare as directed above.

Butter Cookies

 ¾ cup (1½ sticks) butter, softened
 ¼ cup granulated sugar
 ¼ cup packed light brown sugar
 1 egg yolk
 1¾ cups all-purpose flour
 ¾ teaspoon baking powder
 ⅛ teaspoon salt

1. Beat butter, granulated sugar, brown sugar and egg yolk in medium bowl until well blended. Add flour, baking powder and salt; beat until well blended. Cover; refrigerate 4 hours or until firm.

2. Preheat oven to 350°F. Roll out dough on lightly floured surface with lightly floured rolling pin to ¼-inch thickness. Cut into desired shapes with cookie cutters. Place 1-inch apart on ungreased cookie sheets.

3. Bake 8 to 10 minutes or until edges begin to brown. Remove to wire racks; cool completely.   *Makes about 2 dozen cookie*

Chocolate Chip Peanut Butter Cookies

1⅓ cups all-purpose flour
½ teaspoon salt
½ teaspoon baking soda
½ cup granulated sugar
½ cup (1 stick) butter, softened
½ cup creamy peanut butter
¼ cup packed light brown sugar
1 egg, lightly beaten
1 teaspoon vanilla
1 cup semisweet chocolate chips
½ cup peanuts

1. Preheat oven to 350°F. Lightly grease cookie sheets.

2. Combine flour, salt and baking soda in medium bowl. Beat granulated sugar, butter, peanut butter and brown sugar in large bowl with electric mixer at medium speed until light and fluffy. Add egg and vanilla; beat until well blended. Add flour mixture; beat just until blended. Stir in chocolate chips and peanuts.

3. Drop dough by rounded tablespoons 2 inches apart onto prepared cookie sheets.

4. Bake 12 minutes or until edges are lightly browned. Cool on cookie sheets 2 minutes. Remove to wire racks; cool completely.

Makes about 2½ dozen cookie

Oatmeal Hermits

  2 cups quick oats (not instant)
  ½ cup packed brown sugar
  1 cup raisins
1½ cups all-purpose flour
  ½ teaspoon salt
  2 teaspoons baking powder
  1 teaspoon SPICE ISLANDS® Ground Saigon Cinnamon
  ½ cup KARO® Dark Corn Syrup
  ½ cup corn oil
  2 eggs

MIX oats, sugar and raisins in large bowl. Add flour, salt, baking powder and cinnamon; mix well. Whisk together corn syrup, oil and eggs in a small bowl. Add to dry ingredients.

DROP dough by rounded tablespoons 2 inches apart on greased baking sheets.

BAKE 12 to 15 minutes at 375°F until lightly browned around edges. Remove cookies to wire racks to cool.   *Makes 3 dozen cookies*

Prep Time: 10 minutes • Bake Time: 12 to 15 minutes

Smilin' Cookies

1 package (about 16 ounces) refrigerated sugar cookie dough
1 tablespoon plus 1 teaspoon freshly grated lemon peel
   Yellow food coloring
   Yellow decorating sugar
¼ cup semisweet or milk chocolate chips

1. Let dough stand at room temperature about 15 minutes.

2. Beat dough, lemon peel and food coloring, a few drops at a time, in large bowl with electric mixer at medium speed until well blended and evenly colored. Wrap dough in plastic wrap; freeze 30 minutes.

3. Preheat oven to 350°F. Shape dough into 32 balls. Place 2 inches apart on ungreased cookie sheets; flatten into 1¾-inch rounds. Sprinkle with decorating sugar.

4. Bake 9 to 11 minutes or until set. Cool on cookie sheets 2 minutes. Remove to wire racks; cool completely.

5. Place chocolate chips in small resealable food storage bag; seal bag. Microwave on HIGH 1 minute; knead bag lightly. Microwave at 30-second intervals until melted and smooth, kneading bag after each interval. Cut off tiny corner of bag; pipe chocolate onto cookies for eyes and mouths. Let stand until set.   *Makes 32 cookies*

New England Raisin Spice Cookies

1 cup packed brown sugar
½ cup shortening
¼ cup (½ stick) butter
1 egg
⅓ cup molasses
2¼ cups all-purpose flour
2 teaspoons baking soda
1 teaspoon salt
¾ teaspoon ground cinnamon
¼ teaspoon ground ginger
¼ teaspoon ground cloves
⅛ teaspoon ground allspice
1½ cups raisins
Granulated sugar

1. Beat brown sugar, shortening and butter in large bowl with electric mixer at medium speed until creamy. Add egg and molasses; beat until fluffy. Combine flour, baking soda, salt, cinnamon, ginger, cloves and allspice in medium bowl. Stir in raisins. Gradually add shortening mixture, stirring until just blended. Cover; refrigerate 2 hours or until firm.

2. Preheat oven to 350°F. Place granulated sugar in shallow dish. Shape dough into tablespoon-size balls; roll in granulated sugar. Place 2 inches apart on ungreased cookie sheets.

3. Bake 8 minutes or until golden brown. Cool on cookie sheets 1 minute. Remove to wire racks; cool completely.

Makes about 5 dozen cookie

Cranberry Cookies

1 cup (2 sticks) butter
¾ cup packed brown sugar
¼ cup granulated sugar
1 package (4-serving size) vanilla instant pudding and
    pie filling mix
1 teaspoon ground cinnamon
1 teaspoon vanilla
½ teaspoon ground nutmeg
2 eggs
2¼ cups all-purpose flour
1 teaspoon baking soda
1 package (9 ounces) dried cranberries

1. Preheat oven to 350°F.

2. Beat butter, brown sugar, granulated sugar, pudding mix, cinnamon, vanilla and nutmeg in large bowl with electric mixer at medium speed until creamy. Add eggs, one at a time, beating well after each addition. Gradually add flour and baking soda, beating at low speed until blended. Stir in cranberries.

3. Drop dough by rounded teaspoonfuls onto ungreased cookie sheets.

4. Bake 10 to 12 minutes or until golden brown. Remove to wire racks; cool completely. *Makes about 6 dozen cookie*

Snickerdoodles

¾ cup plus 1 tablespoon sugar, divided
2 teaspoons ground cinnamon, divided
1⅓ cups all-purpose flour
1 teaspoon cream of tartar
½ teaspoon baking soda
½ cup (1 stick) butter
1 egg
1 cup (6 ounces) cinnamon baking chips
1 cup raisins (optional)

1. Preheat oven to 400°F. Combine 1 tablespoon sugar and 1 teaspoon cinnamon in small bowl; set aside.

2. Combine flour, remaining 1 teaspoon cinnamon, cream of tartar and baking soda in medium bowl. Beat remaining ¾ cup sugar and butter in large bowl with electric mixer at medium speed until creamy. Add egg; beat until well blended. Gradually add flour mixture to sugar mixture, beating at low speed until stiff dough forms. Stir in cinnamon chips and raisins, if desired.

3. Shape dough into 1-inch balls; roll in cinnamon-sugar mixture. Place 2 inches apart on ungreased cookie sheets.

4. Bake 10 minutes or until set. *Do not overbake.* Remove to wire racks; cool completely. *Makes about 3 dozen cookies*

M&M® Shortbread Cookies

1 cup (2 sticks) butter (no substitutes), softened
½ cup sugar
1 teaspoon SPICE ISLANDS® Pure Vanilla Extract
2 cups all-purpose flour
¼ cup ARGO® Corn Starch
1 to 2 cups M&M's® Chocolate Candies

MIX butter, sugar and vanilla thoroughly using an electric mixer. Gradually blend in flour and corn starch. Stir in 1 cup candies.

FORM into 1-inch balls and place on ungreased baking sheets. Gently flatten each cookie using fingers or a flat-bottomed drinking glass (dipped in sugar to prevent sticking). Press in additional candies to decorate.

BAKE in a preheated 300°F oven for 25 to 30 minutes, or until bottoms begin to brown.

COOL for 5 minutes; remove to wire racks to cool completely.
Makes 3½ dozen cookies

Decorating Tip: Microwave ½ cup semisweet chocolate chips and 1 teaspoon shortening in a small resealable plastic bag on HIGH (100%) power for 30 to 60 seconds, until melted. Snip off corner of bag and drizzle chocolate over cookies. While chocolate is still soft, top with additional candies.

Prep Time: **20 minutes** • Bake Time: **25 to 30 minutes**

Lemon Cream Cheese Cookies

1¾ cups all-purpose flour
½ teaspoon baking soda
½ teaspoon salt
1 cup sugar
½ cup (1 stick) butter, softened
3 ounces cream cheese, softened
1 egg
Grated peel and juice of 1 lemon
½ cup shredded coconut, toasted*
Additional grated lemon peel (optional)

To toast coconut, spread evenly on ungreased cookie sheet. Toast in preheated 350°F oven 5 to 7 minutes, stirring occasionally until light golden brown.

1. Preheat oven to 350°F.

2. Combine flour, baking soda and salt in medium bowl. Beat sugar, butter, cream cheese and egg in large bowl with electric mixer at medium speed until light and fluffy. Add lemon peel and lemon juice; beat until well blended. Stir in flour mixture and coconut; mix well.

3. Drop dough by rounded teaspoonfuls about 2 inches apart onto ungreased cookie sheets.

4. Bake 10 minutes or until set. Cool on cookie sheets 4 minutes. Remove to wire racks; cool completely. Garnish with additional grated lemon peel.   *Makes about 3 dozen cookie*

All-American Chocolate Chip Cookies

2½ cups all-purpose flour
1 teaspoon baking soda
½ teaspoon salt
1 cup (2 sticks) butter, softened
1 cup packed light brown sugar
½ cup granulated sugar
2 eggs
1 tablespoon vanilla
1 package (12 ounces) semisweet chocolate chips
1 cup coarsely chopped walnuts

1. Preheat oven to 350°F.

2. Combine flour, baking soda and salt in medium bowl. Beat butter, brown sugar and granulated sugar in large bowl with electric mixer at medium speed until light and fluffy. Add eggs and vanilla; beat until well blended. Add flour mixture to butter mixture; beat until well blended. Stir in chocolate chips and walnuts.

3. Drop dough by ¼ cupfuls about 3 inches apart onto ungreased cookie sheets.

4. Bake 12 to 14 minutes or until edges are light golden brown. Cool on cookie sheets 2 minutes. Remove to wire racks; cool completely.

Makes about 1½ dozen cookies

Variation: For smaller cookies, preheat oven to 375°F. Prepare dough as directed; drop heaping teaspoonfuls onto ungreased cookie sheets. Bake 8 to 10 minutes or until edges are golden brown. Makes about 6 dozen cookies.

Chocolate Treats

White Chocolate Big Cookies

2½ cups all-purpose flour
1 package (11 ounces) white chocolate chips
1 cup granulated sugar
¾ cup packed brown sugar
¾ cup pecan halves, coarsely chopped
⅔ cup unsweetened cocoa powder
½ cup golden raisins
1 teaspoon baking soda
½ teaspoon salt
1½ cups butter, softened
2 eggs
2 teaspoons vanilla

1. Preheat oven to 350°F. Lightly grease cookie sheets or line with parchment paper.

2. Combine flour, white chocolate chips, granulated sugar, brown sugar, pecans, cocoa, raisins, baking soda and salt in large bowl. Beat butter in separate large bowl with electric mixer until smooth. Add eggs, one at a time, beating well after each addition. Beat in vanilla. (Mixture may appear curdled.) Stir in flour mixture until well blended.

3. Drop dough by ¼ cupfuls about 4 inches apart onto prepared cookie sheets; flatten slightly.

4. Bake 12 to 14 minutes or until firm in center. Cool on cookie sheets 5 minutes. Remove to wire racks; cool completely.

Makes about 2 dozen cookies

Chocolate-Dipped Oat Cookies

   2 cups old-fashioned oats
   ¾ cup packed brown sugar
   ½ cup vegetable oil
   ½ cup finely chopped walnuts
   1 egg
   2 teaspoons grated orange peel
   ¼ teaspoon salt
   1 package (12 ounces) milk chocolate chips

1. Combine oats, brown sugar, oil, walnuts, egg, orange peel and salt in large bowl; mix well. Cover; refrigerate overnight.

2. Preheat oven to 350°F. Lightly grease cookie sheets or line with parchment paper. Shape dough into 1-inch balls. Place 2 inches apart on prepared cookie sheets.

3. Bake 10 minutes or until golden and crisp. Remove to wire racks; cool 10 minutes.

4. Melt chocolate chips in top of double boiler over simmering water. Dip top of each cookie into melted chocolate. Place on waxed paper; let stand until set.   *Makes about 6 dozen cookies*

Mocha Crinkles

1¾ cups all-purpose flour
¾ cup unsweetened cocoa powder
2 teaspoons instant espresso powder or coffee granules
1 teaspoon baking soda
¼ teaspoon salt
⅛ teaspoon black pepper
1⅓ cups packed light brown sugar
½ cup vegetable oil
¼ cup sour cream
1 egg
1 teaspoon vanilla
½ cup powdered sugar

1. Combine flour, cocoa, espresso powder, baking soda, salt and pepper in medium bowl. Beat brown sugar and oil in large bowl with electric mixer at medium speed until well blended. Add sour cream, egg and vanilla; beat until well blended. Add flour mixture; beat until well blended. Cover; refrigerate 3 to 4 hours or until firm.

2. Preheat oven to 350°F. Place powdered sugar in shallow bowl. Shape dough into 1-inch balls; roll in powdered sugar. Place 2 inches apart on ungreased cookie sheets.

3. Bake 10 to 12 minutes or until tops of cookies are firm. *Do not overbake*. Remove to wire racks; cool completely.

Makes about 6 dozen cookie

Fudge-Filled Butter Cookies

   1 cup (2 sticks) butter or margarine, softened
   ½ cup sugar
   1 teaspoon vanilla extract
   2 egg yolks
   2 cups all-purpose flour
   ½ teaspoon baking powder
   ¼ teaspoon salt
   ½ cup HERSHEY®S Mini Chips Semi-Sweet Chocolate
      FUDGE FILLING (recipe follows)

1. Beat butter, sugar, vanilla and egg yolks in large bowl until light and fluffy. Stir together flour, baking powder and salt; gradually add to butter mixture, beating until well blended. Stir in small chocolate chips.

2. Refrigerate about 30 minutes or until firm enough to handle. Meanwhile, prepare FUDGE FILLING. Heat oven to 350°F.

3. Shape dough into 1-inch balls; place 2 inches apart on ungreased cookie sheets. Press thumb in center of each to make indentation; fill with scant teaspoonful filling.

4. Bake 10 to 12 minutes or until light brown around edges. Cool slightly; remove from cookie sheets to wire racks. Cool completely. Store, covered, in refrigerator.   *Makes about 4 dozen cookies*

Fudge Filling

   1 tablespoon sugar
   2 teaspoons cornstarch
   ½ cup whipping cream
   1 egg yolk
   ½ cup HERSHEY®S Mini Chips Semi-Sweet Chocolate
   ½ teaspoon vanilla extract

Stir together sugar and cornstarch in small saucepan; gradually stir in whipping cream. Cook over low heat, stirring constantly, until smooth and thick. Beat egg yolk slightly in small bowl.

tir about 2 tablespoons hot mixture into yolk. Return to saucepan,
tirring until blended. Cook, stirring constantly, just until mixture
omes to a boil. Remove from heat; add small chocolate chips and
anilla, stirring until chips are melted. Cool.

White Chocolate Coconut Delights

12 squares (12 ounces) white chocolate, chopped
 2 cups all-purpose flour
1½ cups flaked coconut, toasted*
 ¾ teaspoon baking soda
 ½ teaspoon salt
 ½ cup packed brown sugar
 ½ cup (1 stick) butter, softened
1¼ teaspoons vanilla
 1 egg
 1 jar (3½ ounces) macadamia nuts, coarsely chopped
    (about ¾ cup)

o toast coconut, spread evenly on ungreased cookie sheet. Toast in preheated 350°F oven
to 7 minutes, stirring occasionally until light golden brown.

Preheat oven to 375°F.

. Microwave half of white chocolate in small microwavable bowl
n MEDIUM-HIGH (70%) 1 minute; stir. Microwave at additional
0- to 15-second intervals until melted and smooth, stirring after
ach interval. Cool slightly.

. Combine flour, coconut, baking soda and salt in medium bowl.
eat brown sugar, butter and vanilla in large bowl with electric mixer
t medium speed until light and fluffy. Add egg; beat until well
lended. Stir in melted white chocolate. Gradually add flour mixture,
eating until well blended. Stir in remaining white chocolate and nuts.

. Drop dough by heaping tablespoonfuls 2 inches apart onto
ngreased cookie sheets.

. Bake 12 minutes or until light golden brown. Cool on cookie sheets
minute. Remove to wire racks; cool completely.

Makes about 3 dozen cookies

Cocoa Snickerdoodles

¾ cup plus 2 tablespoons granulated sugar, divided
¼ cup plus 2 tablespoons unsweetened cocoa powder, divided
2 tablespoons ground cinnamon
2 cups old-fashioned oats
1½ cups all-purpose flour
1 teaspoon baking soda
1 cup butter, softened
¾ cup packed light brown sugar
2 eggs

1. Preheat oven to 375°F. Lightly grease cookie sheets or line with parchment paper. Combine 2 tablespoons granulated sugar, 2 tablespoons cocoa and cinnamon in small bowl; set aside.

2. Combine oats, flour, remaining ¼ cup cocoa and baking soda in medium bowl. Beat butter, remaining ¾ cup granulated sugar and brown sugar in large bowl with electric mixer until light and fluffy. Add eggs, one at a time, beating well after each addition. Stir in oat mixture until blended.

3. Shape dough into teaspoon-size balls; roll in cinnamon mixture. Place 2 inches apart on prepared cookie sheets.

4. Bake 8 to 10 minutes or until firm in center. *Do not overbake.* Remove to wire racks; cool completely.

Makes about 4½ dozen cookie

Black & White Sandwich Cookies

Cookies

    1¼ cups (2½ sticks) butter
     ¾ cup superfine sugar
      1 egg
    1½ teaspoons vanilla
    2⅓ cups all-purpose flour, divided
     ¼ teaspoon salt
     ⅓ cup unsweetened cocoa powder

Filling

     ½ cup (1 stick) butter
      4 ounces cream cheese
      2 cups plus 2 tablespoons powdered sugar
      2 tablespoons unsweetened cocoa powder

1. Beat 1¼ cups butter and superfine sugar in large bowl with electric mixer at medium speed until creamy. Add egg and vanilla; beat until blended. Add 2 cups flour and salt; beat at low speed until blended. Remove half of dough to medium bowl; stir in remaining ⅓ cup flour until blended. Stir ⅓ cup cocoa into remaining dough until blended. Wrap each dough in plastic wrap; refrigerate 30 minutes or until firm.

2. Preheat oven to 350°F. Lightly grease cookie sheets or line with parchment paper. Working with one dough at a time, roll out on lightly floured surface to ¼-inch thickness. Cut out 2-inch circles with cookie cutters. Place 2 inches apart on prepared cookie sheets.

3. Bake 8 to 10 minutes. Remove to wire racks; cool completely.

4. Beat ½ cup butter and cream cheese in medium bowl with electric mixer at medium speed until well blended. Add 2 cups powdered sugar; beat at low speed until creamy. Remove half of filling to small bowl; beat in remaining 2 tablespoons powdered sugar until smooth. Add 2 tablespoons cocoa to remaining mixture; beat until smooth. Spread plain cookies with cocoa filling and chocolate cookies with plain filling. Press cookies together to form sandwiches.

Makes about 2 dozen sandwich cookies

Chocolate-Frosted Marshmallow Cookies

Cookies

- ½ cup (1 stick) butter
- 2 squares (1 ounce each) unsweetened chocolate
- 1 cup packed brown sugar
- 1 egg
- 1 teaspoon vanilla
- ½ teaspoon baking soda
- 1½ cups all-purpose flour
- ½ cup milk
- 1 package (16 ounces) large marshmallows, halved crosswise

Frosting

- ¼ cup (½ stick) butter
- 1½ squares (1½ ounces) unsweetened chocolate
- 1½ cups powdered sugar
- 1 egg white
- 1 teaspoon vanilla

1. Preheat oven to 350°F. Lightly grease cookie sheets. Melt ½ cup butter and 2 squares chocolate in small saucepan over low heat, stirring until smooth. Remove from heat; cool slightly.

2. Beat brown sugar, egg, 1 teaspoon vanilla and baking soda in large bowl with electric mixer at medium speed until light and fluffy. Beat in chocolate mixture and flour until smooth. Beat in milk at low speed until well blended.

3. Drop dough by teaspoonfuls 2 inches apart onto prepared cookie sheets.

4. Bake 10 minutes or until set. Immediately top cookies with 1 halved marshmallow. Bake 1 minute or just until marshmallow is warm enough to stick to cookie. Remove to wire racks; cool completely.

5. Melt ¼ cup butter and 1½ squares chocolate in small saucepan over low heat. Stir in powdered sugar, egg white and 1 teaspoon vanilla, adding a little water, if necessary, to make smooth frosting. Spoon over cookies. Let stand until set. *Makes about 5 dozen cookies*

Extra-Chocolatey Brownie Cookies

2 cups all-purpose flour
½ cup unsweetened Dutch process cocoa powder
1 teaspoon baking soda
¾ teaspoon salt
1 cup (2 sticks) butter, softened
1 cup packed brown sugar
½ cup granulated sugar
2 eggs
2 teaspoons vanilla
1 package (11½ ounces) semisweet chocolate chunks
2 cups coarsely chopped walnuts or pecans

1. Preheat oven to 375°F.

2. Combine flour, cocoa, baking soda and salt in medium bowl. Beat butter in large bowl with electric mixer at medium speed 1 minute or until creamy. Add brown sugar and granulated sugar; beat 2 minutes or until fluffy. Add eggs and vanilla; beat until well blended. Add flour mixture; beat at low speed until blended. Stir in chocolate chunks and walnuts.

3. Drop dough by heaping tablespoonfuls 2 inches apart onto ungreased cookie sheets; flatten slightly.

4. Bake 12 minutes or until set. Cool on cookie sheets 2 minutes. Remove to wire racks; cool completely.

Makes about 3 dozen cooki

Chunky Nut Blondie Drops

2½ cups all-purpose flour
1 teaspoon baking powder
½ teaspoon salt
¼ teaspoon baking soda
1¼ cups packed light brown sugar
1 cup (2 sticks) butter, softened
½ cup granulated sugar
2 eggs
1½ teaspoons vanilla
1½ cups coarsely chopped chocolate squares or nuggets
      with truffle or caramel centers
1¼ cups coarsely chopped pecans, toasted*
1¼ cups coarsely chopped walnuts, toasted*

*To toast nuts, spread in single layer on cookie sheet. Bake in preheated 350°F oven
8 to 10 minutes or until golden brown, stirring frequently.

1. Preheat oven to 350°F. Line cookie sheets with parchment paper.

2. Combine flour, baking powder, salt and baking soda in small bowl.
Beat brown sugar, butter and granulated sugar in large bowl with
electric mixer at medium speed until well blended. Add eggs and
vanilla; beat until well blended. Gradually add flour mixture, beating
well after each addition. Stir in chocolate squares, pecans and
walnuts.

3. Drop dough by rounded tablespoonfuls about 1½ inches apart
onto prepared cookie sheets. (If dough is too soft to handle, cover
and refrigerate 1 hour or until firm.)

4. Bake 15 to 17 minutes or until golden brown. Cool on cookie
sheets 2 minutes. Remove to wire racks; cool completely.

Makes about 4 dozen cookies

Chocolate-Dipped Almond Crescents

　　1 cup powdered sugar
　　1 cup (2 sticks) butter, softened
　　2 egg yolks
　2½ cups all-purpose flour
　1½ teaspoons almond extract
　　1 cup (6 ounces) semisweet chocolate chips

1. Preheat oven to 375°F. Line cookie sheets with parchment paper.

2. Beat powdered sugar, butter and egg yolks in large bowl with electric mixer at medium speed until light and fluffy. Beat in flour and almond extract until well blended.

3. Shape dough into 1-inch balls. (If dough is too soft to handle, cover and refrigerate 1 hour or until firm.) Shape balls into 2-inch ropes, tapering both ends. Curve ropes into crescent shapes. Place 2 inches apart on prepared cookie sheets.

4. Bake 8 to 10 minutes or until set. *Do not overbake.* Remove to wire racks; cool completely.

5. Melt chocolate chips in top of double boiler over simmering water. Dip one end of each crescent in melted chocolate. Place on waxed paper; let stand until set. *Makes about 5 dozen cookies*

Best-Loved Bars

Nutty S'mores Bars

2½ cups graham cracker crumbs (14 crushed whole graham crackers)
1 cup (2 sticks) butter, melted, divided
3 tablespoons sugar
1 package (about 18 ounces) milk chocolate cake mix with pudding in the mix
⅓ cup water
2 eggs
1½ cups mini semisweet chocolate chips, divided
4 whole graham crackers, chopped into ½-inch pieces
1 cup mini marshmallows
1 cup roasted salted peanuts

1. Preheat oven to 350°F. Line 13×9-inch baking pan with foil; spray with nonstick cooking spray.

2. Combine graham cracker crumbs, ½ cup butter and sugar in medium bowl; mix well. Press mixture into bottom of prepared pan. Bake 10 minutes; cool in pan on wire rack.

3. Beat cake mix, remaining ½ cup butter, water and eggs in large bowl with electric mixer at low speed until well blended. Stir in ½ cup chocolate chips. (Batter will be stiff.) Spread evenly over prepared crust. Bake 25 minutes or until toothpick inserted into center comes out clean.

4. Preheat broiler. Sprinkle chopped graham crackers, marshmallow peanuts and remaining 1 cup chocolate chips over bars. Broil 3 minutes or until marshmallows puff and are lightly browned. Cool completely in pan on wire rack. Cut into bars.   *Makes 2 dozen ba*

White Chocolate Mac Nut Berry Bars

1¼ cups all-purpose flour
½ teaspoon baking soda
½ teaspoon salt
1 cup sugar
½ cup (1 stick) unsalted butter, at room temperature
1 egg
1½ cups old-fashioned oats
1 teaspoon vanilla
½ cup sweetened dried cranberries
½ cup white chocolate chips
½ cup macadamia nuts, chopped

1. Preheat oven to 350°F. Spray 8-inch square baking pan with nonstick cooking spray.

2. Combine flour, baking soda and salt in small bowl. Beat sugar and butter in large bowl with electric mixer at medium speed until creamy. Add egg; beat until well blended. Add oats, flour mixture and vanilla; beat 1 minute or just until combined. Stir in cranberries, chocolate chips and nuts. Lightly press mixture into bottom of prepared pan. (Do not compact.)

3. Bake 30 to 35 minutes or until top just begins to brown. Cool completely in pan on wire rack. Cut into bars. *Makes 16 bar*

Double Peanut Butter Paisley Brownies

½ cup (1 stick) butter or margarine, softened
¼ cup REESE'S® Creamy Peanut Butter
1 cup granulated sugar
1 cup packed light brown sugar
3 eggs
1 teaspoon vanilla extract
2 cups all-purpose flour
2 teaspoons baking powder
¼ teaspoon salt
1⅔ cups (10-ounce package) REESE'S® Peanut Butter Chips
½ cup HERSHEY'S Syrup or HERSHEY'S SPECIAL DARK® Syrup

1. Heat oven to 350°F. Grease 13×9×2-inch baking pan.

2. Beat butter and peanut butter in large bowl. Add granulated sugar and brown sugar; beat well. Add eggs, one at a time, beating well after each addition. Blend in vanilla.

3. Stir together flour, baking powder and salt; mix into peanut butter mixture, blending well. Stir in peanut butter chips. Spread half of batter in prepared pan; spoon syrup over top. Carefully top with remaining batter; swirl with metal spatula or knife for marbled effect.

4. Bake 35 to 40 minutes or until lightly browned. Cool completely in pan on wire rack. Cut into squares. *Makes about 36 brownies*

Southern Caramel Apple Bars

   2 cups all-purpose flour
   1 teaspoon salt
   ½ teaspoon baking powder
   ½ teaspoon baking soda
   ⅔ cup butter
   ¾ cup packed light brown sugar
   ½ cup granulated sugar
   1 egg, beaten
   1 teaspoon vanilla
   4 Granny Smith apples, peeled and very coarsely chopped
   24 caramels, unwrapped
   2 tablespoons milk
   ½ cup chopped pecans, toasted*

To toast pecans, spread in single layer on cookie sheet. Bake in preheated 350°F oven 5 to 7 minutes or until golden brown, stirring frequently.

1. Preheat oven to 350°F. Grease 13×9-inch baking dish.

2. Combine flour, salt, baking powder and baking soda in medium bowl. Melt butter in medium saucepan. Remove from heat; stir in brown sugar and granulated sugar. Add egg and vanilla; stir until well blended. Add flour mixture; mix well. Press into bottom of prepared dish; top with apples.

3. Bake 40 to 45 minutes or until edges are browned and pull away from sides of pan. Cool completely in pan on wire rack.

4. Heat caramels and milk in medium saucepan over medium-low heat until caramels are melted and mixture is smooth, stirring constantly.

5. Drizzle caramel sauce over bars; sprinkle with pecans. Let stand 30 minutes or until set. Cut into bars.   *Makes about 2 dozen ba*

Rocky Road Crispy Treats

6 tablespoons butter
2 packages (10 ounces each) large marshmallows
1 package (12 ounces) semisweet chocolate chips, divided
1 box (13½ ounces) crisp rice cereal
1 package (6 ounces) sliced almonds, divided
2 cups mini marshmallows

1. Spray 13×9-inch baking pan with nonstick cooking spray.

2. Melt butter in large saucepan over low heat. Stir in large marshmallows until melted and smooth. Stir in 1 cup chocolate chips until melted. Remove from heat; stir in cereal. Stir in remaining 1 cup chocolate chips, 1 cup almonds and mini marshmallows.

3. Press mixture into prepared pan. Sprinkle with remaining ⅔ cup almonds. Let stand until set. Cut into bars. Store in airtight container up to 1 day.
Makes about 2 dozen bars

Seven-Layer Dessert

½ cup (1 stick) butter, melted
1 teaspoon vanilla
1 cup graham cracker crumbs
1 cup butterscotch chips
1 cup chocolate chips
1 cup shredded coconut
1 cup nuts
1 can (14 ounces) sweetened condensed milk

1. Preheat oven to 350°F.

2. Combine butter and vanilla 13×9-inch baking dish, tilting pan to distribute evenly. Sprinkle evenly with graham cracker crumbs. Layer with butterscotch chips, chocolate chips, coconut and nuts. Pour sweetened condensed milk over layers.

3. Bake 25 minutes or until lightly browned. Cool completely in pan on wire rack. Cut into bars.
Makes about 2 dozen bars

Chewy Butterscotch Brownies

2½ cups all-purpose flour
1 teaspoon baking powder
½ teaspoon salt
1 cup (2 sticks) butter or margarine, softened
1¾ cups packed brown sugar
1 tablespoon vanilla extract
2 large eggs
1⅔ cups (11-ounce package) NESTLÉ® TOLL HOUSE®
   Butterscotch Flavored Morsels, divided
1 cup chopped nuts

PREHEAT oven to 350°F.

COMBINE flour, baking powder and salt in medium bowl. Beat butter, sugar and vanilla extract in large mixer bowl until creamy. Beat in eggs. Gradually beat in flour mixture. Stir in *1 cup* morsels and nuts. Spread into ungreased 13×9-inch baking pan. Sprinkle with *remaining ⅔ cup* morsels.

BAKE for 30 to 40 minutes or until wooden pick inserted in center comes out clean. Cool in pan on wire rack. Cut into bars.

Makes about 2 dozen brownies

Prep Time: 12 minutes • Baking Time: 30 minutes

White Chocolate Blondies

      2 cups old-fashioned oats
      1 cup all-purpose flour
      1 cup packed brown sugar
      1 cup white chocolate chips
      1 teaspoon baking powder
      1 teaspoon baking soda
      1 teaspoon salt
    ¼ cup (½ stick) unsalted butter, softened
      2 eggs
    ½ cup sweetened condensed milk
      1 teaspoon vanilla

1. Preheat oven to 350°F. Grease 9-inch square baking pan.

2. Combine oats, flour, brown sugar, white chocolate chips, baking powder, baking soda and salt in large bowl. Beat in butter until well blended. Beat in eggs, sweetened condensed milk and vanilla until well blended. Press mixture into prepared pan.

3. Bake 25 to 30 minutes or until toothpick inserted into center comes out clean. Cool completely in pan on wire rack. Cut into bars.

Makes 25 ba

Tangy Lemon Raspberry Bars

¾ cup packed light brown sugar
½ cup (1 stick) butter, softened
   Grated peel of 1 lemon
1 cup all-purpose flour
1 cup old-fashioned oats
1 teaspoon baking powder
½ teaspoon salt
½ cup raspberry jam

1. Preheat oven to 350°F. Spray 8-inch square baking pan with nonstick cooking spray.

2. Beat brown sugar, butter and lemon peel in large bowl with electric mixer at medium speed until creamy. Add flour, oats, baking powder and salt; beat at low speed until well blended. Reserve ¼ cup mixture. Press remaining mixture into prepared pan. Spread evenly with jam; sprinkle with reserved mixture.

3. Bake 25 minutes or until edges are lightly brown. Cool completel in pan on wire rack. Cut into bars. *Makes 16 ba*

Chocolate Caramel Pecan Bars

2 cups butter, softened and divided
½ cup granulated sugar, divided
1 egg
2¾ cups all-purpose flour
⅔ cup packed light brown sugar
¼ cup light corn syrup
2½ cups coarsely chopped pecans
1 cup semisweet chocolate chips

1. Preheat oven to 375°F. Grease 15×10-inch jelly-roll pan.

2. Beat 1 cup butter and granulated sugar in large bowl with electric mixer at medium speed until light and fluffy. Add egg; beat until well blended. Add flour; beat at low speed until just blended. Spread evenly in prepared pan. Bake 20 minutes or until light golden brown.

3. Meanwhile, bring remaining 1 cup butter, brown sugar and corn syrup to a boil in medium heavy saucepan over medium heat, stirring frequently. Boil 2 minutes. *Do not stir.* Stir in pecans; spread evenly over prepared crust.

4. Bake 20 minutes or until dark golden brown and bubbling. Immediately sprinkle with chocolate chips. Cool completely in pan on wire rack. Cut into bars.

Makes 40 bars

Chocolate Chip Cookie Bars

¾ cup granulated sugar
¾ cup packed brown sugar
½ cup (1 stick) butter, softened
½ cup shortening
2 eggs
1 teaspoon vanilla
2½ cups all-purpose flour
1 teaspoon baking soda
1 teaspoon salt
2 cups (12 ounces) semisweet chocolate chips
1 cup chopped pecans or walnuts

1. Preheat oven to 375°F. Grease 13×9-inch baking dish.

2. Beat granulated sugar, brown sugar, butter and shortening in large bowl with electric mixer at medium speed 3 minutes or until creamy. Add eggs and vanilla; beat 2 minutes or until well blended. Add flour, baking soda and salt; beat at low speed until well blended. Stir in chocolate chips and pecans. Spread evenly in prepared dish.

3. Bake 20 minutes or until golden brown and firm. Cool completely in pan on wire rack. Cut into bars. *Makes 1½ to 2 dozen bar*

Variations: Substitute peanut butter chips, milk chocolate chips or raspberry-flavored chips for half or all of the semisweet chocolate chips.

Oat and Apricot Bars

1½ cups all-purpose flour
1½ cups old-fashioned oats
　1 cup packed brown sugar
1½ teaspoons ground cinnamon
　½ teaspoon salt
　½ teaspoon baking soda
　½ cup vegetable oil
　¼ cup apple juice
　1 cup apricot preserves or apricot fruit spread

1. Preheat oven to 325°F. Grease 13×9-inch baking pan.

2. Combine flour, oats, brown sugar, cinnamon, salt and baking sod
in large bowl. Combine oil and apple juice in small bowl; stir into flou
mixture just until moistened. Reserve 1¼ cups oat mixture; press
remaining oat mixture evenly into prepared pan. Spread evenly
with preserves; sprinkle with reserved oat mixture.

3. Bake 35 minutes or until golden brown. Cool completely in pan c
wire rack. Cut into bars.　　　　　　　　*Makes about 2 dozen ba*

Holiday Delights

Valentine Kisses

    2 egg whites
      Pinch cream of tartar
    ½ cup sugar
      Pink or red food coloring

1. Preheat oven to 250°F. Line cookie sheets with parchment paper.

2. Beat egg whites in medium bowl with electric mixer at medium-high speed until foamy. Add cream of tartar; beat until soft peaks form. Add sugar, 2 tablespoons at a time, beating until stiff and glossy. Stir in food coloring until batter is dark pink. (Color will lighten during baking, so batter should be darker than desired shade of pink.)

3. Drop meringue by tablespoonfuls 1 inch apart onto prepared cookie sheets. (Or pipe 1-inch mounds of meringue using pastry bag fitted with large writing tip.)

4. Bake 30 minutes or until firm. Turn oven off; let cookies stand in oven 1 hour. Remove from oven; cool completely.

Makes about 5 dozen cookies

Chocolate Chip Valentine Kisses: Prepare recipe as directed, gently folding in ¾ cup mini semisweet chocolate chips just before adding the food coloring.

Linzer Sandwich Cookies

1⅔ cups all-purpose flour
¼ teaspoon baking powder
¼ teaspoon salt
¾ cup granulated sugar
½ cup (1 stick) butter, softened
1 egg
1 teaspoon vanilla
Powdered sugar
Seedless red raspberry jam

1. Combine flour, baking powder and salt in small bowl. Beat granulated sugar and butter in medium bowl with electric mixer at medium speed until light and fluffy. Add egg and vanilla; beat until well blended. Gradually add flour mixture, beating at low speed until dough forms. Divide dough in half. Wrap each half in plastic wrap; refrigerate 2 hours or until firm.

2. Preheat oven to 375°F. Working with one half at a time, roll out dough on lightly floured surface to ¼-inch thickness. Cut dough into desired shapes with floured cookie cutters, cutting equal numbers of each shape. (If dough becomes too soft to handle, refrigerate 10 minutes or until firm.) Cut 1-inch centers out of half of each shape. Place cutouts 1½ to 2 inches apart on ungreased cookie sheets. Reroll centers and trimmings; repeat cutting shapes as directed above.

3. Bake 7 to 9 minutes or until edges are lightly browned. Cool on cookie sheets 1 to 2 minutes. Remove to wire racks; cool completely.

4. Sprinkle cookies with holes with powdered sugar. Spread jam on flat sides of whole cookies, spreading almost to edges. Place cookies with holes over jam to make sandwiches.

Makes about 2 dozen sandwich cookie

White Chocolate Shamrocks

2 packages (about 16 ounces each) refrigerated sugar
    cookie dough
½ cup all-purpose flour
    Green food coloring
1 package (14 ounces) white chocolate candy discs
    Green and white sprinkles, dragées or decorating sugar

1. Let doughs stand at room temperature about 15 minutes.

2. Preheat oven to 350°F. Lightly grease cookie sheets.

3. Beat doughs, flour and food coloring, a few drops at a time, in large bowl with electric mixer at medium speed until well blended and evenly colored.

4. Roll out dough between sheets of parchment paper to ¼-inch thickness. Cut out shapes using 2-inch shamrock cookie cutter. Place 2 inches apart on prepared cookie sheets. Refrigerate 15 minutes.

5. Bake 8 to 10 minutes or until set. Cool on cookie sheets 5 minute Remove to wire racks; cool completely.

6. Microwave candy discs in medium microwavable bowl on HIGH 1 minute; stir. Microwave at additional 15-second intervals until melted and smooth, stirring after each interval. Dip edges of each cookie into melted chocolate. Place on waxed paper; decorate with sprinkles. Let stand until set.   *Makes about 2 dozen cookie*

Decadent Coconut Macaroons

1 package (14 ounces) flaked coconut
¾ cup sugar
6 tablespoons all-purpose flour
¼ teaspoon salt
4 egg whites
1 teaspoon vanilla
1 cup (6 ounces) semisweet or bittersweet chocolate chips, melted

1. Preheat oven to 325°F. Line cookie sheets with parchment paper or grease and dust with flour.

2. Combine coconut, sugar, flour and salt in large bowl; mix well. Add egg whites and vanilla; beat until well blended.

3. Drop batter by tablespoonfuls 2 inches apart onto prepared cookie sheets.

4. Bake 20 minutes or until set and light golden brown. Remove to wire racks; cool completely.

5. Dip macaroons in melted chocolate. Place on waxed paper; let stand until set.

Makes about 3 dozen macaroons

Eggs-Cellent Easter Cookies

1 package (about 16 ounces) refrigerated sugar cookie dough
¼ cup all-purpose flour
1 cup plus 1 tablespoon powdered sugar, divided
1 teaspoon almond extract
Green food coloring
1 package (3 ounces) cream cheese, softened
1 tablespoon butter, softened
Red food coloring
½ cup shredded coconut
Colored decorating icings and gels

1. Let dough stand at room temperature about 15 minutes.

2. Preheat oven to 350°F. Grease cookie sheets.

3. Beat dough, flour, 1 tablespoon powdered sugar, almond extract and green food coloring, a few drops at a time, in large bowl with electric mixer at medium speed until well blended and evenly colored.

4. Shape dough into 2½-inch egg shapes. Place 2 inches apart on prepared cookie sheets.

5. Bake 8 to 10 minutes or until set and edges are lightly browned. Cool on cookie sheets 2 minutes. Remove to wire racks; cool completely.

6. Beat cream cheese, butter, remaining 1 cup powdered sugar and red food coloring, a few drops at a time, in medium bowl with electric mixer at medium speed until smooth and evenly colored. Stir in coconut.

7. Spread pink filling on flat sides of half of cookies. Top with remaining half of cookies to make sandwiches. Decorate tops of sandwiches with decorating icings and gels as desired. Let stand until set. Store in refrigerator.   *Makes 1½ to 2 dozen sandwich cookies*

NESTLÉ® TOLL HOUSE®
Stars and Stripes Cookies

1 package (16.5 ounces) NESTLÉ® TOLL HOUSE®
   Refrigerated Chocolate Chip Cookie Bar Dough
1 package (8 ounces) light cream cheese (Neufchâtel),
   at room temperature
⅓ cup granulated sugar
24 fresh, medium strawberries, sliced
¾ cup fresh blueberries
2 tablespoons NESTLÉ® TOLL HOUSE® Semi-Sweet
   Chocolate Mini Morsels

PREHEAT oven to 350°F.

ROLL cookie dough to ¼-inch thickness between two pieces of wax paper. Remove top piece of paper. Cut cookie dough into stars with 3-inch star cookie cutter. Transfer cookies to ungreased baking sheet(s). (If stars are too hard to remove from wax paper, refrigerate rolled dough for 10 minutes.) Roll remaining dough to ¼-inch thickness; cut out additional stars.

BAKE for 10 to 12 minutes or until light golden brown. While hot, reshape and pat edges of each star back into shape with knife. Cool on baking sheet(s) for 2 minutes; remove to wire rack(s) to cool completely.

BEAT cream cheese and sugar in small mixer bowl until fluffy. Spread onto cooled cookies. Place strawberry slices onto each cookie pointing outward. Place 5 to 6 blueberries in center of each cookie. Top each cookie with morsels.   *Makes 20 cookies*

Prep Time: 15 minutes • Cooking Time: 10 minutes • Cooling Time: 5 minutes

Harvest Pumpkin Cookies

2 cups all-purpose flour
1 teaspoon baking powder
1 teaspoon ground cinnamon
½ teaspoon baking soda
½ teaspoon salt
½ teaspoon ground allspice
1 cup sugar
1 cup (2 sticks) butter, softened
1 cup solid-pack pumpkin
1 egg
1 teaspoon vanilla
1 cup chopped pecans
1 cup dried cranberries or raisins
Pecan halves (about 36)

1. Preheat oven to 375°F.

2. Combine flour, baking powder, cinnamon, baking soda, salt and allspice in medium bowl. Beat sugar and butter in large bowl with electric mixer at medium speed until light and fluffy. Add pumpkin, egg and vanilla; beat until well blended. Gradually add flour mixture, beating at low speed until well blended. Stir in chopped pecans and cranberries.

3. Drop dough by heaping tablespoonfuls 2 inches apart onto ungreased cookie sheets; flatten slightly. Press 1 pecan half into center of each cookie.

4. Bake 10 to 12 minutes or until golden brown. Cool on cookie sheets 1 minute. Remove to wire racks; cool completely.

Makes about 3 dozen cookie

Sugar & Spice Halloween Cookies

2⅓ cups all-purpose flour
2 teaspoons ground cinnamon
1½ teaspoons baking powder
1½ teaspoons ground ginger
½ teaspoon salt
¼ teaspoon ground nutmeg
¾ cup (1½ sticks) butter, softened
½ cup packed brown sugar
½ cup molasses
1 egg
Colored frostings and decorating sugars

1. Combine flour, cinnamon, baking powder, ginger, salt and nutmeg in medium bowl. Beat butter and brown sugar in large bowl with electric mixer at medium speed until light and fluffy. Add molasses and egg; beat until well blended. Gradually add flour mixture, beating just until combined. Shape dough into two discs. Wrap in plastic wrap; refrigerate 1 hour or until firm. (Dough may be prepared up to 2 days before baking.)

2. Let doughs stand at room temperature about 15 minutes.

3. Preheat oven to 350°F. Roll out doughs on lightly floured surface to ¼-inch thickness. Cut out shapes with 2-inch Halloween cookie cutters. Place 2 inches apart on ungreased cookie sheets.

4. Bake 12 to 14 minutes or until centers of cookies are firm. Cool on cookie sheets 1 minute. Remove to wire racks; cool completely. Decorate with frostings and decorating sugars as desired.

Makes about 2½ dozen cookie

Rugelach

1½ cups all-purpose flour
¼ teaspoon salt
¼ teaspoon baking soda
½ cup (1 stick) butter, softened
1 package (3 ounces) cream cheese, softened
⅓ cup plus ¼ cup granulated sugar, divided
1 teaspoon grated lemon peel, divided
1 cup ground toasted walnuts*
1 teaspoon ground cinnamon
2 tablespoons honey
1 tablespoon lemon juice
Powdered sugar

To toast walnuts, spread in single layer on ungreased baking sheet; bake in preheated 350°F oven 8 to 10 minutes or until golden brown, stirring frequently. Remove walnuts from baking sheet to cool. To grind walnuts, place in food processor; process using on/off pulsing action until ground, but not pasty.

1. Combine flour, salt and baking soda in small bowl. Beat butter, cream cheese, ⅓ cup sugar and ½ teaspoon lemon peel in large bowl with electric mixer at medium speed 5 minutes or until light and fluffy. Gradually add flour mixture, beating at low speed until well blended. Shape dough into three discs. Wrap doughs in plastic wrap; refrigerate 2 hours or until firm.

2. Preheat oven to 375°F. Grease cookie sheets. Combine walnuts, remaining ¼ cup sugar and cinnamon in medium bowl. Combine honey, remaining ½ teaspoon lemon peel and lemon juice in small bowl.

3. Working with one disc at a time, roll out dough on lightly floured surface with lightly floured rolling pin to 10-inch circle. (Keep remaining dough refrigerated.) Brush dough with one third of honey mixture. Sprinkle with ⅓ cup nut mixture, lightly pressing into dough.

4. Cut dough into 12 triangles with pizza cutter or sharp knife. Beginning with wide end of triangle, tightly roll up. Place 1 inch apart on prepared cookie sheets. Repeat with remaining dough, honey mixture and nut mixture.

5. Bake 10 to 12 minutes or until light golden brown. Cool on cookie sheets 1 minute. Remove to wire racks; cool completely. Sprinkle with powdered sugar.

Makes 36 cookies

Eggnog Cookies

2¼ cups all-purpose flour
  1 teaspoon baking powder
  1 teaspoon ground cinnamon
  1 teaspoon freshly grated nutmeg
1¼ cups sugar
  ¾ cup (1½ sticks) unsalted butter, softened
  ½ cup eggnog (alcohol-free)
  2 egg yolks
  1 teaspoon vanilla
    Additional freshly grated nutmeg

1. Preheat oven to 300°F.

2. Combine flour, baking powder, cinnamon and nutmeg in medium bowl. Beat sugar and butter in large bowl with electric mixer at medium speed until light and fluffy. Beat in eggnog, egg yolks and vanilla. Gradually add flour mixture, beating at low speed until well blended after each addition.

3. Drop dough by rounded teaspoonfuls 2 inches apart onto ungreased cookie sheets. Sprinkle with additional nutmeg.

4. Bake 20 minutes or until bottoms are lightly browned. Cool on cookie sheets 2 minutes. Remove to wire racks; cool completely.

Makes about 4 dozen cookies

Tip: Whole nutmeg seed pods and mini graters are available in the supermarket spice section.

Holiday Peppermint Slices

1 package (about 16 ounces) refrigerated sugar cookie dough
¼ teaspoon peppermint extract, divided
  Red food coloring
  Green food coloring

1. Let dough stand at room temperature about 15 minutes.

2. Combine one third of dough, ⅛ teaspoon peppermint extract and enough red food coloring to make dough desired shade of red. Knead dough until evenly tinted.

3. Repeat with second one third of dough, remaining ⅛ teaspoon peppermint extract and green food coloring.

4. Shape each portion of dough into 8-inch log. Place red log beside green log; lightly press together. Place plain log on top. Press logs together to form one tri-colored log. Wrap in plastic wrap; refrigerate 2 hours or until firm.

5. Preheat oven to 350°F. Cut log into ¼-inch-thick slices. Place 2 inches apart on ungreased cookie sheets.

6. Bake 8 to 9 minutes or until set. *Do not overbake*. Cool on cookie sheets 1 minute. Remove to wire racks; cool completely.

Makes about 2½ dozen cookies

Cherry Snowballs

2¼ cups all-purpose flour
1½ cups powdered sugar, divided
¾ cup chopped pecans
⅔ cup dried cherries
¼ teaspoon salt
1 cup (2 sticks) butter, softened
1 teaspoon vanilla

1. Combine flour, ½ cup powdered sugar, pecans, cherries and salt in food processor; process until nuts and cherries are finely chopped. Add butter and vanilla; process until dough forms. Wrap dough in plastic wrap; refrigerate 30 minutes.

2. Preheat oven to 400°F. Line cookie sheets with parchment paper. Roll dough into 1-inch balls; place 1 inch apart on prepared cookie sheets.

3. Bake 10 to 12 minutes or until set. Cool on cookie sheets 5 minutes.

4. Meanwhile, place remaining 1 cup powdered sugar in large resealable food storage bag. Add a few cookies; seal bag. Toss gently to coat. Repeat with remaining cookies. Remove to wire racks; cool completely. *Makes about 4 dozen cookie*

Acknowledgments

The publisher would like to thank the companies listed below for the use of their recipes and photographs in this publication.

ACH Food Companies, Inc.

The Hershey Company

Nestlé USA